A Second Whisper

for Dannie

A Second Whisper

Lynne Hjelmgaard

Seren is the book imprint of
Poetry Wales Press Ltd.
57 Nolton Street, Bridgend, Wales, CF31 3AE
www.serenbooks.com
facebook.com/SerenBooks
twitter@SerenBooks

The right of Lynne Hjelmgaard to be identified as
the author of this work has been asserted in accordance
with the Copyright, Designs and Patents Act, 1988.

ISBN: 978-1-78172-554-2
ebook: 978-1-78172-560-3
Kindle: 978-1-78172-561-0

A CIP record for this title is available from the British Library.

The publisher acknowledges the financial assistance of the Welsh Books Council.

Cover painting: by Jan Petersen – egg tempera

Author photograph: Jane Allan

Printed in Bembo by Latimer Trend & Company Ltd, Plymouth.

Contents

Introduction: The Empress of Odessa

Starving, at L'artista, I ate my whole plate of Pasta ai Funghi. Surprised, you said 'Kinahora' (the kid knows how to eat). Yiddish. I hadn't heard that word since childhood. After lunch you read from *The Presence* and poems about silence. You had asked me to read my own poems of loss. Later, dazed, I got on the wrong train. We discovered a shared Jewish heritage: your brother Leo, MP; my grandfather Leo, trumpet player from Odessa; my mother Katherine, mathematician; your much-loved mother, Kate. A cousin Frieda, an aunt Frieda, other common stories of loss: uncles, cousins, aunts, our fathers, mothers and you, during the war. We also shared our grief for respective spouses from long, happy marriages. And for a time it was the four of us. Though one day, without ceremony, we noted their absence.

It felt like I had joined a large family, especially when I week-ended at your house: the photographs of your wife Joan, children and grand-children, an enormous poetry library, calligraphies of your framed poems, paintings by well-known artists, poetry friends you introduced me to. The much-travelled suitcase I used between your house and mine, packing and unpacking weekly, is gone now. (When we met I invited you, joking-ly, to come along.) You didn't feel the need to travel except to see Cardiff City games. Weekly letters and invitations to read your poetry meant you rarely had to venture far from Hodford Road. The world came to you. After a while you insisted, when some festival or venue called, that Lynne Hjelmgaard read her poems too or you wouldn't come. You were moved by my genuine happiness for your good reviews. I was moved when you gave me your yellow rose in front of the crowd at Hay.

Joan wanted to throw away a suede coat you had brought back from a teaching year at Princeton in the 70s. She thought it was old and ragged, was probably right. But I quickly adopted it, especially on frosty nights in your cold kitchen where you cooked meals and had the table ready on Friday nights to welcome me home. There was our age difference: the Kosher butcher asking, 'How's your father?' Your worry I'd meet some-one younger; my fear of your impending death – you, a healthy eighty-five. After a few years you bought me a ring: a delicate amethyst stone we chose together to mark a relationship we couldn't explain, just felt, deeply.

Your nosy neighbour at the front door, 'Who is this woman?' And your deadpan reply, 'The Empress of Odessa.' There was no clear path ahead, only the present we forged on Golders Green Road, our Champs-Elysées, our meetings with wherever poetry and Eros chose to take us.

Speak to Me Again at Dusk

Speak to me again at dusk
and once again at dawn.

Your volcanic green hills
and pungent honey smell

open a dark place
like a cloud that lifts.

It opens with the sweet lapping
of water on a rock

and closes gently where the tide
has nowhere to run.

These lines among many lines
are words just for you

and the roosters that speak them
just before dawn.

It Was the Day They Put the Clocks Back

Torbay Station

'Time was away and somewhere else.'
                    Louis MacNiece

Minutes were not wasted with you dear Poet,
          who called himself a Welshman and a Jew –

whose elder charm and youthful spirit rose
          in the excitement of the rush.

We drank our builder's tea at the platform café
          busy speaking of our past lives

when the waitress removed the clock…
          In the train back to London

we sat shoulder to shoulder, poem to poem.
          The girl in the seat across the aisle

watched us intently, her gaze and smile
          lingered longer on yours.

I hardly knew you, yet had pangs of jealousy and
          still in grief for my own lost spouse, later wrote:

give me him young or give me him old,
          is he writing me now as I write of him?

The Gift

Out front, unknowing passers-by
can't see the many books you gave me
arranged on my living room floor.

In alphabetical order they wait
to be placed on shelves; the musty scent
of letters and notes I find in old ones,
the shine and glorious covers of the new.

I think of the study they came from, yours,
still homesick for the home that no longer is.
Where are we then placed in the world?

Now a year on I've lost the sense
of being able to conjure you up,
honey smells of your room, vines
from the apple tree that grew through walls

(you refused to cut them back),
the door stop that never stayed put,
springs in the leather couch that finally gave way.

Would you want to be here?
Now on cool autumn evenings,
glow of yellow leaf, glow of yellow lamp,
dusk then darkness,

birdsong dwindles as if birds are being tucked in
by night air and knowing
inner worlds of the houses they sing to.

A Second Whisper

When I leave the house
there is a palpable darkness hovering.
Light pretends to be sun. Earth inhabits
another fragile year, constellations engulf us.

Who among us does not think better when alone?
The baby magpie, little trollop, still has its baby fat,
too heavy to fly. Yet it takes a few steps, flaps its wings,
attempts take-off. Stops and starts again and again.

In the riverboat an egret and goose wait patiently,
side by side. Waiting as if their will alone
will take them across. What better way to hide than
in the company of another who also hides.

Aged and dying you grew more tender,
wanting to leave. The house helped me let you.
I knew just how to open your front door quietly.
Its lock a whisper, a second whisper to shut.

This Is Where You Come to Me

when we still had our afternoons
        next to the vine we couldn't name

where the boy in the fountain leans back
        juggling two fish in his hands

their mouths wide open
        gasping for breath

where the yew
        twists in and out

like limbs of lovers
        curling inwards spiralling up

where spray from the water jet chills
        and the sun on my shoulder burns

It Felt Foreign at First

It felt foreign at first
        as if I had never spoken it,

dreamed it
        and now I sometimes forget

I had a beloved
        in you.

And that there can be more
        to reach for,

a feeling of lightness that was,
        is here still

and in itself becomes
        more mine, purposeful.

I return
        to conversations, language,

when our widowed worlds
        first connected,

when you said,
        'Come back tomorrow, stay'.

At the Event

He looks proud standing next to the younger woman
     who's less sure of herself; she's not used to
          the attention he seems comfortable with.

What was he saying just before the camera man interrupted,
     just before the click of the lens?
          He could've been talking about anything

and she would listen because he always listens to her,
     their arms linked; his head tilted
          drawing her in, their eyes intensely focused

on a poem, a book, each other. He reaches for her hands,
     reassures her, cracks a joke and so she smiles
          cautiously as the camera pulls them along.

Afterthoughts

The taxi driver asks, 'Where is he the old poet?'
When I tell him he pulls out one of his own love poems
(in a frenzy) and quickly translates on a whim.

I don't understand a word
but his broken English
draws me in like the song

of the sad sparrow that coaxed you away
and the robin that brought you back
to our favourite bench in the park.

I thought how good it would have been if we could have
experienced 'the rampart of rain and the bottomless moat of thunder'
together under skies of such changing moods.

When your absence is most intense
your abridged postcard versions (that you
re-named Post-Card-iffs) make me laugh:

Dangerous Curves
(yours not Peter Cheney's)

The Company She Keeps
(may it be me)

Tender is the night
(when we are together)

I sent you a Little Mermaid card
from Copenhagen and wrote:

She was on loan to China
who one time lost an arm
and two times lost her head...

At Villa Borghese

Rome 2007

How many times in life does a peacock cross your path?

A fountain trickles down a narrow flight of stairs.
I put my hands in the cool to become cleansed and hopeful
like the man singing an aria at the entrance to the park.

The vegetable man cracks a smile with no front teeth.
A one-legged beggar smells of urine in the sun,
where men take his money beside the Spanish Steps.

On the terrace a man sitting next to me
doesn't meet my eyes. He eats his spaghetti,
napkin neatly tucked in his collar, twirls his pasta
around his fork without once looking up.

The poet (he's a poet because of the curious way
his suspenders hold his trousers up), arranges papers
and notebooks on a bench.

Lovers mingle on the grass, their legs intertwined
next to busts of handsome Italian men: Ugo,
Giuseppe, Leonardo, Raphael.

Each of us fall into separate dream-states in the shade.
Piazza del Popolo is steaming.
The sirocco comforts us on the top of the hill.

The postcard you hadn't sent me yet,
because I hadn't met you yet said:

'Just before the sun went down
the angels sounded like birds.'

Visitor

The night you introduced yourself the scent of lilacs
lingered in the ground after rain.

You were like a summons from another world,
full of longing and joy –

a soothing presence coaxing me out
of a deep sleep with your melodious tenor.

Is it the nectar that lured you to the garden,
the damp soil, an open window?

Is it love to want to be part of your passing dream,
your sad ancient spirit in a bird?

Listen to me, take me there
so we can celebrate

fresh green shoots sprouting
on the bare trunks of the lime tree together.

With Dannie

for what seems like hours
we stood under the awning
on Golders Green Road
the harder it rained
the longer we waited
whenever it rains
now or anywhere the rain
stops everything
to think of you

A Thief Is in the House

I hear his heavy breathing

    as he runs up the stairs

to find you waiting

    patiently in bed.

Your head propped on pillows

    your eyes prepared

for nothingness

    in the dimly lit room.

Into a whirlwind

    the house disappears.

Green, Green I love you Green

During my walks on the Heath
I hear you in the silence:

Green, Green I love you Green,

as I fondle an envelope
addressed to us both.

Three Tree Poem

Planted on either side of the garden
they slowly inch their way closer
until finally (a century or two later)
the fir leans into its beloved palm.

The lonely tamarisk has roots
tough enough to grow through rocks;
it waits until it can drink
from the bay eighty feet below.

Instructions for the Coastal Walk
from Clarach to Borth

When you realize it's too late to turn back
give a good yell! There is no one around.

Squat. Slide slowly down the steep parts
on your bum. Take deep breaths.

Watch out for the barbed wire on your right
and the long drop off the cliff on your left.

Be comforted by the sweet faces of cows.
They don't know what a burger is.

Ignore the to-the-top-of-your-head
hammer pounding in your ears.

Cry out to your loved ones who are dead.
They won't hear you – but you'll feel closer to them

when you glare down at the abyss.
Listen to the surf crashing on the beach.

The breaking up and letting go.
It has a kind of seeing without eyes.

And your whole body knows this.
And your whole body knows this.

To a Chestnut Tree

late autumn

There will always be another one.
And another one.

Loss can be moved through like a room.

I want to put leaves back on your branches,
give the dead back their years.

(Even if we don't know who they are,
they are housed among us.)

I hope this letter's not too late.

Nature can topple buildings,
erase mankind with one blast,

so hungry it is at times
for the true spirit of our beginnings.

On Willow Road

Outside my window a wild parakeet
occupies a branch upside down.

We understand each other: our need
for comfort, seeds and play.

Its lime-green tail shoots straight up
like the sword of a dancer,

an acrobat, a jester's headstand
in the courtly game of seek and ye shall find.

It teases me through the glass
as if I were looking out from the edge

of a hollow in the bark.
I will it to come closer

just as I will the ash tree's buds to burst.
Always slow, always last.

London, Forever Tired in Your Arms

I want to sleep soundly like the two Asian
workers on the train who lean on each other.

Splattered paint on their hair and trousers,
they allow London to take care of them

and, for the moment, London does.
I even stop, contemplate their history,

the latest disastrous headline in my face.
These grown-up babes-in-arms,

seemingly secure here in this dark,
steely underworld of tracks.

Hampstead Poem

I see him
from my kitchen
window,

his study
faces it, beneath
the chestnut

and my window
just across,
opposite the tree.

He seems to take
refuge behind
a rose bush

that has grown
tall and wide,
to shield more of

his person.
I think there
are moments

he hides
so we both
can hide.

When I glimpse
the top of
his bald head

I try not
to sneak away,
instinctively

I want to.
Don't care
to be seen

early, first thing
when feeling
vulnerable,

mind fragmented
by dreams or
too little sleep.

I discover a way
of placing
my cup

slantwise
on the counter edge.
This oddness

of being
watched or not,
by a man

who hides
or not,
behind a rose

bush framing
his study window,
ceremoniously

placed beneath
the tree,
we share.

Living in London

No-see-ums. Hello to the invisible,
always hearable footsteps. At night
when I lie in bed (theirs just above mine),
I hear a thud. A lost shoe? A fallen book?

Or an odd closet creak, a hurried walk
across, a miles-away muffled voice.
6:30 am, another thud. We get out of bed,
the wakeful three-some. Quick

to shut the alarm clock, turn on
the tap, run the shower, brew the tea.
I make sure they can't see my light
on their way down. I do not want them

to know me, other than my bike and mud–
caked wellies parked outside my door.
Only when they are gone do I speak.
No-see-ums… Hello.

The Couple Downstairs

'…the god of Not-Yet looks on'
Jane Hirschfield

Only the back room with a soft angle of light
        through the glass as a suggestion.

Only the dark door and the dark front room
        where the voices are that I never see.

Not during the day when the main door slams,
        or late evening

when I'm already in bed,
        when their joyful cries begin.

Sleepless, I turn to photographs of my lost beloveds
        and tell them:

Not-yet-dead, not-yet-lost, not-yet-taken.

Rhea Americana

Golders Hill Park

I spy you in the far off, it's nearly spring.
Bird chatter, daffodils still hibernating,
slowly coming out of it. I walk further
into the park. Walk the hill in the light rain.

My pages are wet, the ink smudges
with expectations. You raise your head.
Your too-small-for-your-body-head, placed on
your totem-pole neck, like an afterthought.

You move closer. I can almost touch
your small feminine ears, layers of feathery tutu.
Blank eyes stare into nothingness as if
there is still some unknown hurt

lurking under the grass. We stand here
nearly motionless until you tip-toe away
back to your hiding place behind a shrub.
Have I disappointed you?

Keepsakes/A Prism

I have a small, carved wooden box with a few keepsakes inside, one
of them being a prism stolen from a chandelier in 1969, from the main
hall of Monmouth College, West Long Branch, New Jersey, around
dinnertime, during the month of March.

It was stolen a few months before four students were shot dead at Kent
State. Before several friends of mine were arrested in a drug bust, had all
their hair cut off in the local jail. Before it was suddenly the end 'of life
as we knew it' on college campuses across the country.

The prism was taken, at my urging, by my boyfriend, Paul Zwicker,
who was visiting me from Rutgers. That night I snuck him into my
dorm room (before co-ed dorms existed there). What I remember,
most vividly, is that he had to pee in a coke bottle, or was it 7up? and
that we'd empty it from time to time out the window, trying not
to make any noise.

We'd gaze up at the night sky from our mattress on the floor,
listen to the Incredible String Band while making love and afterwards
admire our prism on the windowsill. We'd hold it up against the
moonlight, behold its blurry kaleidoscopic world inside of a world
that we could bend and shape with our eyes, disappear into,
make our own with just the turn of a hand.

I can't remember how Paul was able to steal the prism. How did
he reach it, was there no one around to stop us, did he climb up
on a chair? Why did I want him to take it even? Why have I saved it?
But now, as I write this, I remember holding my breath with excitement
as he took it and that exhilarating sense of HA! as we ran out of the
beautiful main hall.

I remember the hall, a mansion with fresco-like paintings of angels
on the ceiling and a large, winding staircase. I can still hear the voices
that quietly echoed off the walls and floor-to-ceiling windows. In the
distance the early evening light danced through fir trees on the terrace.
The nerve of it all. I wanted that prism.

So it has its place in the box next to my daughter's broken pink coral necklace, my son's first baby tooth and a few conkers that were placed in his bed by mischievous friends on his wedding night. There is also a handkerchief from my dear friend Norrie. I've lost touch with her. Norrie, my first friend in poetry.

Ode to Blue Jeans

You are the engine that rules –
full throttle!

Ragged or faded
puckered or pressed

a tight-lipped fit hug-
ing the crotch and hip

or loose around the knees
with a faulty zip.

Dressed-down to slouch
dressed-up to thrill

when we put you on
we don't sit still.

       ★

Your fagged-out odour
of denim and sweat

soaks the cagey man
standing in the aisle.

He slow-steps past us
in the daily coach

his backside crack
airs for a while.

All the others smile
for him to pull you up.

But I smile for him
to pull you down.

Ladybirds

Like a group of older women
who gather unnoticed

in a dance hall
counting heads, guessing ages

and wounds from afar,
they stake their claim silently

to be near each other,
inch along the same ceiling,

spots on a skyline
in one corner

of a garden flat.
Later, outside, their hard shells

are trampled on,
they no longer have wings

or are found
lying on their backs.

Writer's Retreat

Vermont

Instead of sitting in the main house
        emailing and gossiping

or working
        alone in our rooms, one night

we older women
        circle around and around

in Nancy's car
        before venturing inside

The Long Trail Pool Saloon.
        And suddenly I'm aware –

Kathy
        has tears in her eyes.

You, Lizard-like

expert at loss, loyal to none,
slip into unknown spaces, claws
digging quickly in, out. You disappear
between things and survive.

Can never go back yet alter course;
are a foreigner in your own company,
who can fade into the dimness of a room
and still be there. Dutiful to darkness.

You hear and seek, see and hide.
Light colours your inner world
as the outer one changes. How quickly
you can flee and shed your skin.

Innocently unfaithful to mate or nest.

Death in the Taverna

Chickens cackle behind a thin curtain
        that divides the room.
At first the thud thud
        in the background
is subtle, some one or some thing –
        chopping, hacking.

There are white tablecloths;
        glued to the wall
        is a smiling, moustachioed
portrait of a man.
        His meagre 1930's pre-war
profile peers back

        amid a display
of knives, tongs, saws.
        All those fear-sodden birds
the owner must have butchered –
        necks and breasts and thighs:
        thud, chop chop.

A sweaty silhouette appears
        to take our orders. He resembles
his forefather but doesn't have
        the lean face or
        delicately pointed twirl
at the end of his moustache –

that takes a gentle hand
to achieve. He doesn't
      say much, does it
         with his body: clap–slam,
whack, a broom across the floor
      in one sweep.

He stops to gloat
      at beauty
contestants on the screen.
      Chicken–chat.
Slap-bang.
      Hissing-hot. Meat.

Stone and Spider

I dragged you both home
in a heavily packed suitcase:
the snail in you, Stone,

is a centimetre wide
dating back 60 million years
(or so the Cretan scientist said).

You, Spider, already busy
making yourself at home –
I love the quiet of your labour.

Here's to long friendship,
passion for life deeply lived
and anonymous (and amorous)
corners in which to grow.

In Gainsborough Gardens

I return to the tree that still stands

– beautiful, haunted, dead.

Why does it thrill me? Tall beheaded creature –

the more I return the more comforting

it becomes, yet not a leaf or branch grows there

just clusters of knobby holes,

pock-mocked scabs on bark.

Before I admired only what was alive

and green, but now it draws me in wondering

what kind of tree stands here

no longer of this world yet in it –

looming dark, majestic, holy.

Holy as in prayer, as singing

is prayer or memory shooting

crooked angles to the sky.

The Brooklyn Bridge, a Fish-foul Smell of the East River, Grey

1

Get directions from the parked police car,
follow tiny whirlpools in the dirty tide,
heart longing for a boat ride,
for hot humid city days and water sprinklers
from the past, ask how's Brooklyn
on the other side now? The steel girders,
whizzing sound of various metal
working against metal, a passing inhalation
of gas stink (used to love that smell),
fumes of fresh tar, hard pavement,
scraped knees from childhood.
Follow the river down past the iconic view,
jets in the air grid to JFK and further,
further than the horizon can reach itself.
Further than the rain.

I once sailed under that bridge,
left the city willingly, happily free
and following green buoys out to sea.
Didn't steer too close to the edge of the channel
where swift currents could take you
and freighters and tugboats have right of way.
I kept my watch. Faithful to the helm,
always hungry, always sleepy,
often wet and having to pee.
Watched out for flotsam, debris:
a lone barrel from a freighter
could hole a ship, a thick line or rope
could get caught in the screws,
we'd lose steering, drift, end on the rocks.

A distorted floating shape at 11 o'clock
could be a dead body, speaking of which...
we were ordered to circle a corpse
by the Coast Guard until they arrived
and wrapped dissolving flesh in chains.
Iron links straddled what remained of skin
and bone, tied it alongside their ship,
barely lifting it out of the water
as they moved along, barely blinking an eye.

2

Manhattan is a chain with many links,
some are broken, lost and never repair,
but others can be retrieved even at a distance.
For what can shine so brightly at sea
but a city, once loved, left behind?
There are many who live on the streets.
But for all its harshness it still feels like
an old friend, even in unknown Brooklyn
neighbourhoods or Gucci Armani neighbourhoods.
It leads the way when I'm lost in the subway
where an angry woman rants solo
against the world on the F train.
She is standing very close, close enough
to smell her breath, feel her wrath.
Her eyes take me hostage
until we reach the next stop
when a gentle person seated just across
takes her by the hand and leads her away.

Mother

When I think of you
I think of bridges

a body of water

of how many times
I tried to cross over

How you once held the map
so seemingly secure
but in truth
even as a child
I sensed your unease

(you didn't know
you didn't know
where we were going)

But who can blame you

trying to walk the distance,
a limited portion of water
cupped in your hands?

Winter Gives Me...

Winter gives me permission to shut down,
to crawl inside myself and rest.

Winter is twenty-four hours when
I can travel the furthest –

live inside a Hammershøi,
a snow-covered cityscape

or deep in the woods
soundless as my neighbour upstairs.

I only hear his footsteps,
even his dog Snoops, a quiet,

sweet-faced spaniel, never barks.
I don't know much about dogs,

have never owned or even liked them
except for Frieda, my son's dog.

She sits at his feet when he writes
at his desk, follows him everywhere –

Frieda. Frieda! except when he travels.
Living far away and rootless

as he is, there is this nagging feeling.
It can pull me apart and throw me

back together again just like that.
I know nothing about parental love.

My Daughter Tries to Reach Me on the Phone

The river enters the house and everything goes,
including the two-person beige Ikea sofa

and big pillows that haven't turned up in years;
the sleeveless knit dress bought for the festivities

and the only decent chair Aunt Frieda can sit on.
Meanwhile no one at the party shuts the door

that would stop the flood. They stand at
the bar together, laughing and talking. Even

cousin Ronnie, the bald accountant who used to live
in New York, and Joseph who ran for Mayor

and didn't win and doesn't drink anymore.
Soon after they took a freighter to the South Pole

and were never heard from again. And...

Berith

I haven't written enough about you
and the many times I think of doing it
I seem to push you away
to the far-off corner of my desk
not deliberately
but because I take you for granted
you are always with me
or with some part of me
that isn't separate
we share a space continuously together
unconsciously without effort
without having to explain much
only to hear our own sound
briefly is enough
the sound we are for each other
oh yes you are there
I am here
yet when you first came along
I was too young
to understand or even think about
what is a mother
I just became one for you
as you have said from time to time
especially when we were younger
are you really my mother
you questioned my whole being
my youth my oddness
different than what you expected
or maybe hoped for
when you said Mom
now it's difficult for me to comprehend
where the mother ends
and the daughter begins
but of course you are here
and I am here

In a Sailing Dinghy with Berith

Cardigan Bay

The bay we were in could have been
the anchorage we knew from home
coming back to us – its smell
like seaweed and crabs and jellyfish,
        if jellyfish have a smell…

        How docile
our harbour used to be
at low tide when we would catch
the launch that ferried us to shore
and sometimes spy an occasional rat or two
slipping into a crevice in the rocks.

Berith said she'd work the sails.
I sat at the tiller but couldn't
get the feel of it right,
kept pointing the boat wrong,
kept heading into the wind
        (where's the weathervane,
        where's the wind?)

Inevitably the boom came crashing over
but we were safe and we were laughing;
        and the more I struggled
        the harder we laughed
at near misses with other boats,
crashes into buoys, tangled lines,
billowing sails filling with water,
land moving further and further away.

The Exchange

for Kim

Child as I used to know him,
not so much as he is now,
a loving father.

He's disappeared into a vastness
as if he'd walked away
without looking back.

The immediacy of his presence
in my mind fluctuates, recedes
like a piano sonata, learned

and listened to. Then the foot off
the pedal, the slow fading,
hush of quiet, letting go of sounds.

As a young mother
I couldn't have perceived
love's later roadblocks:

distances and silences,
lengthy measured pauses
or wrong notes;

the many times we would
slight each other blindly,
just by being who we were.

My Children Walk Ahead

My children walk ahead, each one holds
    a dog on a lead.

Parents now, brother and sister,
    almost the same height,

several years apart. Middle-aged.
    They chat and joke together.

When we reach the park, they let the dogs
    run loose, circle each other,

play-biting, teasing, barking. Two dark furry shapes
    gallop, jump and roll on the grass.

My children swing the leads, twist them around
    their hands. I keep my distance,

watch them from behind. This is also love.
    When we get further into the park

the space between us broadens
    until at some point they are very far away.

Bully in the Playground

How the lady cradled tough Jimmy
when he cracked his head,

held him in her arms and ran
and all of us ran after,

blood streaming out of his head
and how she tried to stop it

with her shirt, a rag, her eyes,
we all tried to stop the blood

with our eyes. Watching and
running and watching

his blood, his cracked head,
wanting Jimmy to get home.

Soper's Hole

Tortola, March 1985

How calm the water is
that has taken the boy

how piercing the screams
of the mother in the no-wind

in the stillness of the birds
Not a breath in the harbour

for anyone and in the screams
that carry across the water

as the father's hands work
trying to bring the boy back

For days and weeks afterwards
the harbour itself is dead

How like not-being-alive we are
fearing birds and water and air

that stole the child quickly
with a lift of the surge

ONCE

for Hanne

Like different species
of birds perched
on separate branches

of the very same tree,
we see each other
without seeing

each other,
and can only hear
our own song.

When we talk, she is
elsewhere, on a foreign,
unlit street.

She's kissed my new-born,
rubbed the feet
of my dying husband,

slept next to me
in my empty bed,
a new widow.

We consoled each other
when we learnt
our spouses weren't perfection,

rocked our babies to sleep,
scolded each other – too much,
too little.

I once knew how to
lay her breakfast table,
toast her bread,

knew her mother's
embroidered tablecloths,
the royal porcelain

in the heirloom chest,
candlesticks on the sill
lined up, just so.

Thoughts and secrets
laid bare, opened as easily
as jam jars

in the kitchen,
studied like
detailed maps,

lost treasures
brought forth
from our chests –

aired, unguarded,
slippery as warm butter
on our knives.

Now we write careful letters
as if they are to lost versions
of ourselves.

The men understand
up to a point – until their eyes
glaze over and

acquire that far-away look.
Other times behind
closed doors,

they overreact
like wild boars
trapped in a bush

until suddenly released
without clearly knowing
whom or what to attack.

Pieve a Castello

An extra bolt on the door, a small square window
    in the eaves, a wooden ladder
        placed underneath, just so.

Outside in the hall, one heavy stone step was removed
    long ago, when there were warnings…
        and downstairs a skull

unearthed here, glistens behind glass. What else
    has been woven into pastoral scenes
        on these woollen walls –

what love has been here, what lives lost
    folded in like a dark thought. By day cypresses seem benign
        lining country lanes, by night

their tall dark shadows bend and lurk like serpents,
    conspirators twisting and turning
        every nightmare's whim. But tomorrow

I will wait for the soft hooting owl around sunset
    and night sky that protects it. And later
        I will open my window

to watch for signs of life at a house across the fields
    where they say no one lives. I will wait for flapping wings
    of bats as they circle the lemon tree,

hills, woods and vineyards. I will listen to the gentle
    chanting air and not be afraid
        to let the darkness seep in.

Ode to a Danish Lamp

When I walk down the stairs you are waiting for me.
You've had enough of the night and long shadows,
the curtains are drawn. We're in the depths
of dark November and a silence at 6 am.
My fingers can feel along the wall
until they find your switch.
As a mere human I can't measure up
to your Nordic metallic cool,
your graceful subtle orbit – a lamp composed
solely for the pleasure of the seeing eye.

I am humbled to have a seat beside you right now
and for the foreseeable future. We exist together
in this space containing us, filled with books, knickknacks,
tables and chairs. I move my belongings around until
I find the right position for every object in the room
or until it finds its place or the place finds it
at the appropriate distance from you.

A cracked royal porcelain vase
has the ability to inch forward and
mirror back, residing next to the photos
on the shelf as long as it likes,
as proof of a life and the many lives
once connected, as you and I are connected
by the wizard electrician who talks to himself
in the terminology of the wire.
Who finds answers in his own questions
as he goes along, like he's recording a voice
from deep within, in a language
only he can understand (and maybe you).

Because he hooks you up
to the charged interior, a territory,
where no country nationality race
or religion has any significance.
Because here we are placed, have identity
and form without having to dig too deeply,
journey far or escape for long or be anything other
than what we discover in the symphony of you
under your fine, oh so thin aluminium rim.
In the faint circular hue of purple only visible
when seated (closely) below. In the faint circular
hint of red only visible when standing (closely) above.

Why do you move me so?

Mountains at Sea

for Stig

Once the seas started to build
it could take days

for them to subside
and the more they grew

the more I could sense
the turning point

they brought you to –
which couldn't be found otherwise

this turning – and the calm
it contained for you.

27th and 6th

If I were to write honestly, I would write about
my fear of staying in one place
and the first time we packed a suitcase together.
Can't remember what we packed,
what clothes we had, I think not many.
Didn't know the journey would be ongoing:
mostly together, from our first place of abode –
the loft we shared with Ray and Gopalbhai on 27th and 6th
above the prostitutes who tried to pick our pockets
when we walked up the stairs and below the noisy beat band
and ceiling that shook every time they played.
The ceiling you plastered with different coloured paper,
our own true map of the world.

Degnemøse Alle

Copenhagen, 1971

after our long journey I lie down for a nap
    in the room off the garden
        hearing the faint murmur of voices

outside the window   your voice
    speaking a language I haven't yet learned
        rises and falls with much to tell

after years away returning home
    the listeners intent on listening
        happy is the news

and I am part of the news
    there's strangeness but also comfort
        in the high-pitched chirp of sparrows

tulips from your mother's garden
    she's already put in the vase
        next to our bed

I sit up to grasp the softness   warmth
    safety of this place like when I felt
        I knew you before I knew you

Ellinge Lyng

I used to venture out alone most days
        knowing you were close by, knowing
                these woods, this cabin near the sea.

In the autumn standing under the trees in the rain,
        no one else on the path, just the scent of
                dead leaves, fresh pine and the hush.

Or walking stubbornly out into a winter storm,
        snow drifts higher than I can remember,
                determined to get a glimpse, if only

for a few moments – the vast whiteness, angry breaking waves,
        frozen sand. Then getting stuck – each foot
                weighed down by the snow as I tried to lift it.

My craving is still for quiet, the same time each evening,
        a single paragraph, the intimacy of reading Thoreau.
                When a deer crossed the road just before dark

it was so quick and soundless, my first thought: a shadow
        is trailing behind me. It could have been you –
                why come back I ask?

But I do. I walk along the edge of the water
        where I used to gather mussels and clams, just to gaze
                across the bay, just to walk there.

I Can Almost Sense the Divide

I'm not sure where the hunger comes from
      or what kind of hunger it is or why

you are dying in the hospice room I keep wanting to fill with things,
      make myself larger, make you *not* go away.

But if I move in with my books, if I fill the room,
      become larger…

The windows are high and not for looking out,
      the light is sharp and bright.

Outside there is movement in the leaves at the very tops of the birch trees –
      but you are busy looking elsewhere – at what only the dying can see.

At one point you get up and sit in a chair. Then you speak
      in a voice so clear for what it knows

observing us, our life together
      as someone moving on.

As We Silently Agree

'…when you want nothing
from this human world'
>> from *Off-Hand Chant*
>> Po Chü-i

Now, in some kind of afterlife
you paint the anchor chain –

a marker at every meter.
You're still in your wedding clothes

in the shirt you always wore:
a sky-dyed blue.

You watch the other ships –
where are they going,

what have they left behind
and will their anchors drift tonight?

Below, you search the ship's log:
sun sights, daily positions,

how many miles to go.
Weathered charts are tossed about –

torn on their yellowed edges,
cracked with age in their folds.

They are spread out and studied
under the keen light

of your sailor's eye.
But where can they take you?

Our fingers clasp in recognition
as we silently agree:

what does it matter now
if you don't keep the course?

Scorpion Hill

Sometimes, at sunset, I return to our house in a small boat.
      It glides easily across the channel, the song of tree frogs
            following with the evening wind.

Other times getting across is like trying to ride a wet bull
      without a saddle, thighs clinging to its back,
          hands struggling for grab holds in the cockpit,

spray hitting hard – biting hard – a slap across the face.
      Why go back there to share the company of vermin and ghosts?
         Where there are echoes of conversations: you walking
towards me

to put the kettle on or to pour a glass of red
      complaining about bites from the no-see-ums; where rats chew
         on window screens or squeeze through cracks

in the cupboard, teeth marks left on apples and soap.
      Loud rattling doors that never locked, can't shut,
         scorpions disappear into hiding places.

Outside a cluster of moths, all shapes and disguises,
      wings fluttering, cling to a single light bulb
         left on during the night.

Acknowledgements

My thanks to the editors of the following publications and websites where these poems have appeared including *Poetry Wales, PN Review, The Guardian, London Grip, Acumen, Artemis* and *Fanfare: Poems by Contemporary Women Poets.*

Thank you to the writers whose words appeared as epigraphs or italicized lines in some of these poems: Jane Hirschfield, D.H. Lawrence, Federico Garcia Lorca, Kei Miller, Louis MacNeice, Po Chü-i and Dannie Abse.

I am indebted to Jane Duran and Mimi Khalvati for their encouragement at the beginning stages of the manuscript, their insight, careful reading and helpful comments. I am also grateful to Alice Notley, Gillian Clarke, Lawrence Scott and to my fellow writers in the Wednesday night group and monthly Sunday afternoon group; also to Norbert Hirschhorn, Wendy French and Nora Hughes.

The artwork on the cover is by my dear friend and collaborator the Danish Artist Jan Petersen, who allowed me to use his painting on this cover and whose work has graced several of my book covers through the years.

My warm thanks to my editor Amy Wack and everyone at Seren for their patience, understanding, support and hard work.

And once again thank you and with love to my children Berith and Kim, and my grandchildren: Finn, August, Maris, Conor and Mia.

And always Stig.

About the Author

Lynne Hjelmgaard, born in NYC, has three published poetry collections: *Manhattan Sonnets* (Redbeck Press, 2003), *The Ring* (Shearsman, 2011) and *A Boat Called Annalise*, (Seren 2016). She moved to Denmark with her husband to raise a family in the 70's and at one point, sailed across the Atlantic and lived for a while in the Caribbean (a journey detailed in her previous collection, *A Boat Called Annalise*. She is presently working on a sequence of responses to the poems of Dannie Abse.